1982

(W)HOLES

ALFRED A. KNOPF

NEW YORK

1980

(W) H O L E S

POEMS BY

CYNTHIA MACDONALD

THIS IS A BORZOI BOOK
PUBLISHED BY ALFRED A. KNOPF, INC.

Some of these poems have appeared in
*The Georgia Review, Parnassus, The New Yorker,
Pruning the Annuals, Hair-Raising,* and *Shenandoah.*
"Burying the Babies" first appeared in
The North American Review.

LIBRARY OF CONGRESS CATALOGING IN PUBLICATION DATA
Macdonald, Cynthia.
(W)holes.
I. Title.
PS3563.A276W5   1980   811'.5'4   79-2298
ISBN 0-394-50852-1
ISBN 0-394-73751-2 pbk.

Manufactured in the United States of America
FIRST EDITION

For my loves of twenty-three and twenty years,
Jennifer Tim and Scott Thurston,
and to my new love, M. S.

Thanks to the New York State Council on the Arts for a CAPS grant, to the Yaddo Corporation for a tranquil place to work, to the Rockefeller Foundation for an Aspen Institute for Humanistic Studies fellowship, and to Susan Crile for her help in arriving at an order. Special thanks to my fellow artists in the National Academy and Institute of Arts and Letters: the award you gave me in recognition of my writing enabled me to finish this book more coherently.

CONTENTS

I

~

This symbol indicates space
between sections of a poem
wherever such spaces are not
apparent due to page breaks.

I

"*Nothing is ever the same as they said it was.
It's what I've never seen before that I recognize.*"

DIANE ARBUS

FRANCIS BACON (1561–1626; 1910—), THE INVENTOR OF SPECTACLES, IS THE RINGMASTER

ALL MOUTH

I.

It was all mouth; only
The frill of flesh around the lips and
The rudimentary bag might have been considered
Differentiated tissue.

The mouth part was perfect
And was exhibited—the bag hidden beneath—
On a blue velvet cushion to emphasize
This was a patriotic display.
During sideshow hours it would play
"Columbia, the Gem of the Ocean" on its kazoo
And mouth slogans like
"A slip of the lip may sink a ship."

There was a lot of argument about its sex.
Experts said, "Female, that's obvious,"
But when it stuck out its tongue to show what it thought
Of experts, some changed their minds and said,
    "Androgynous."
All Mouth did not care what they said;
It would eat anything.

2.

All Mouth's pregnancy was difficult.
It did not like to sunbathe
Or swim at the pool or beach;
It was embarrassed about the bulge of its bag.
But it needed water all the time, needed immersion to
Cool. None of the circus administrators
Could understand why it shunned public swimming
When it took to its pillow each night without a murmur
And would gladly stick its tongue in ink to autograph
Photographs. But its kin knew that displaying
Your triple hump or the fountains in your aorta or
Your elephant skin or your star-spangled vulva in the sideshow
Did not mean you could bare it outside.

3.

All Mouth had given birth to part of what it lacked
And kept All Ear close night and day,
Rocking it on the rim of the cradle
Which all ears have built in, savoring its pet name,
Ma petite oreille, whispering secrets to it,
Caressing its intricate passages.

> Sleep, little baby ear.
> All Mouth will sing you to sleep
> With Brahms and charms

And Edward Lear,
Blue Boy and Little Bo-Peep.

ALL EAR, *twenty years later*

    I.

It was off to the side, off center.
It tried to sing, All Mouth its model.

    Hear me, hear me;
    Take me inside you.
    I would make waves of sound rise and ebb in you
    Till your climax swamps you and you drown,
    Brahms doughy, Ravel liquid.
    Let me stuff your cunt with slick explosions,
    Let me enfold you in the circle of my flesh.

But All Ear, only receptive, made no more sound
Than a windless wind tunnel.

    2.

All Ear willed its transformation.
It smelled a little, but it wouldn't
Give two cents to become a nose:
Such narrow circles, really ovals,
And pipes without tunes.

3.

Ear, hear, he, her, hearing,
Unheard. All Ear's frustration mounted.
Using its own stirrup,
It rode words like an empty boat,
Lashed itself with words of need unmet,
Irritation and hate until
A drop of blood formed;
More, until a stream circled its canals,
Circled red around its hole,
A whirlpool, an iris.

The ringmaster flicked his whip,
Honoring the ire of what once had been
The ear, and in the twinkling of one,
The eye, the new star, was spotlighted in
The Black Tent of Marvels, Mysteries and Wonders,
An Amazing Gallery of Actually Forty
Beautiful, Living, Blended Supernatural Visions.

ALL EYE

1.

Hurry, hurry, hurry
To see the *Italian*,
The third in the Eye, Ear, Nose and Throat team.

See its spaghetti tears;
Listen when I pinch it, it will go *ai, ai, ai*.
("What do you mean, lady, didn't you ever hear of
A Jewish *I*talian?") And I'm going to ask you, little girl,
"What does an *I*talian wear to a masked ball?"
"Mascara."

2.

All Eye, which had been staring at the sky, closes its lid
To close out the peripheral circus,
To follow the sun's blue afterlife
Diagonally up and across the red air. Blue off the edge,
Trailing fainter suns as the lid sky deepens
To purple, then black.

3.

The eye is the most courageous organ because, in a sense,
It must always face itself. It lies in its moist socket,
The pot of seeing, and never says that what it sees in dream
Is less than what it sees. Image and imagination,
Those eyes indivisible.
In the deep of my eye, I see
To the edge of self (all those translucent pronouns)
And beyond into the dark quarter of the circle.

THE WORLD'S FATTEST DANCER

She stands in the lake of her fat,
Lean as the center pole in the main tent.
And then she is off, pirouetting sharply,
Pleating the air with the needle of
Her toe. She has completed
Almost three hundred pliés before the first
Wave appears on the placid lake.

Nureyev will try almost anything, but found
Lifting her more than trying.
They are not sure if his spine will ever
Snap back, won't know till
He gets out of traction. She visits him,
Bringing consolations of
Chocolates and larded guinea hens.

Whoever dances with her, she is
The biggest attraction:
Spangles, bright as egret eyes,
Colors, oily as peacock-feather eyes:
All eyes are upon her.
When she performs The Dying Swan, they
Borrow from the *Guinness Book* and
Bring on a piano case as her coffin:
That is the scale on which she founders.

~

It is difficult to understand
Her words because her mouth is very
Small, a spidery *Water Stick* on
The glistening lake.
And though her public adores and
Adorns her with flowers or, sometimes,
Emeralds and tourmalines,
No one can nibble a kiss.

THE MOTHER OF THE SUN

He was born the sun. Hair (yes, his inheritance),
Golden corona, face, flat and luminous.
"A clock," said the nurse
Holding him up by his hands,
But the doctor, who knew the family, said,
"No. The sun." They named him Ray, the Sun Prince,
Because Sonnenheim was wrong for exhibition:
"Behold the sun, living like ordinary royalty,
Taking a bath. Sleeping. Eating his floating island."

He was impossible to hold.
His mother, who loved him most,
Who knew that her light would come from him after
His father died, could not resist him
And her arms and breasts were covered with burns.

Finally she had to leave him; she had her own
Course to follow. The Rival Circus insisted,
Ignoring her protest that she would be
Nothing without reflection, a sequin in the dark.
They had bought her contract and wanted
Their Queen Diane.
All she could do was lie, pale on the table like
A grey plate, no matter
How much gold lamé they surrounded her with.

Until the day he brought his baby to see her:
The son of the sun.
When she bent to kiss him,

The years of separation had lowered her resistance
And she caught fire, burning, a new meteor
Trailing blue and
Orange ribbons of flame. She burned her way
Right through the tobacco canvas of the main tent
And ignited the night sky over
The western Sun Belt like a match on black paper.

In five minutes she had almost devoured herself
And went out, leaving only splinters which
Would fall some day like knives into
The earth. The father threw his son up in
The air, saying, "My mother is there, playing
Hide and seek,
Waiting for you. Kiss
The sky. Maybe she will come back to us."

But she hid behind a veil of milk;
The star of her own show.

THE SIAMESE SEXTUPLETS

Ten years ago the Siamese sextuplets
Were cut apart to form heroic couplets.
(Such surgery is swift: an S-shaped cut
Where the zeniths of the ribs abut.)
Enlistment followed in the New Crusades;
Garbed in gold, they led the Pope's parades;
The lines of men arrayed in holy order,
Attacking, before attacked, the heretic border.
The couplets' uncut legs, like diamond posts,
Sparkling with strength to serve the heavenly hosts,
Flashed through the air of war, then in encampments
Wore velvet shoes to soften their enjambments.

And all of this because of six made three,
Boned and cut into paired filigree.
The severed bliss of being simply paired,
Of double-sharing what was once six-shared:
To stand as two, to sit as two, to leap,
To meet, to eat as two and when asleep
To sleep as two. At cockcrow to make love
As four . . . The pairs give praise to Heaven above:
Three pairs beneath the ribs of the Cathedral,
Three pairs give thanks for being ditriahedral.

Well-versed on freedom and on what impinges,
The twins went into war like well-oiled hinges.
They were such heroes on the battlement
That all the stars within the firmament

Repaired their fraying light and cleansed the span
Of sky to make a black silk space. Now scan
Past Ursa Major, past the Milky Way:
The Trinity of Six turns night to day;
The severed Thaïs adorn the branchy reaches,
Brighter than diamonds sparkling wet on Alexandrine beaches.

We struggle, fingering our scars, through the damp sand of indecision
Awaiting the meteors, the release, the embrace, the collision.

CELEBRATING THE FREAK

for May Swenson

The freak is	the other
The freak is	wrapped in lamb cloth because
It is precious	
The freak is	precious
The freak is	the other
Alarming us	when it talks through the crook in its arm as it has no mouth
Astounding us	when it threads its legless, armless body through the eye of a needle
Amazing us	when it plays a violin concerto with its feet
The German freak	replaces vaccine for the Germans
The Finnish freak	swims the Baltic for the Finns
The Armenian freak	disarms the cruelest Armenians
The Polish freak	is a totem for the Poles
The freak wears	well
Though it dies early	
The freak wears	silk and velvet to promote its nobility
The freak wears	on the outside what we conceal
The freak wears	down. It becomes tired of being
The freak. It retires	to a country home built to its
Freak specifications:	low toilets or moving staircases or beds the size of billiard tables
The freak leaves us	bereft, forcing a little
Mutilation somewhere	to set things right
To wreak	penance
To set	the freak flags flying.

THE KILGORE RANGERETTE WHOSE
LIFE WAS RUINED

There we were that beautiful line, synchronized as
A row of pistons in an Eldorado, except
There are only eight of them and there were a hundred of us
(Flowers weeded out of flowers, the cream of the crop).
There we were in the Cotton Bowl, the world-famous
Kilgore Rangerettes, kicking to "The Eyes of Texas Are Upon You"
And they were. In our white cowhide skirts and white felt hats
And red satin shirts and vests with silver stars and
I kicked with the wrong leg and the heel of
My white patent boot got caught in Marybelle's heel on the right
And we both fell and knocked into
The girls on either side of us who sprawled into
Others and half the line went down
Like a keyboard in a demo derby whacked by an axe.

Maybe I should have known—there had been
Problems of appearances before:

Hugging Grandma too tight after she'd had her surgery.
She held the empty place and cried.
Grandpa said she loves you; be more careful.
He bought me a grey suede bag to keep things in.

Giggling in my Hark the Herald Angels Sing duet,
Infecting my partner, too.
The principal said we ruined the Christmas Concert.
My father gave me a garnet and emerald
Synthastone pin in the shape of a clef.

~

Having a nosebleed when I was shaking hands with
The head of Pan American who came for dinner.
A drop fell on his tan pants.
My father didn't get promoted
But he said that wasn't why.
My mother gave me a box of linen handkerchiefs
Embroidered Monday, Tuesday, Wednesday . . .

Not only did I have to leave the Rangerettes
I left Kilgore, too, even though my roommate,
Who'd been the Maid of Cotton, told me she still loved me.
My intended said the same and gave me
A satin slip, but I don't know . . .
I felt he shouldn't have a ruined wife.
It was that way with any good job, too.
How could I work in the fine crystal section at Neiman's?
All those long-stemmed goblets. Cascades of glass chimes
Woke me every night. I asked to be transferred to
Sterling and Gems. But the tines, the blades, the facets
Menaced me. I learned you break or are broken.
And then a Texaco receptionist, Jack-In-The-Box waitress . . .
No need to spell the perils out.

They know me in Dallas—the only bag lady—lots in NYC—
But all of them are old and I am not. I saw them
On a Kilgore trip to catch the Rockettes and the Balanchine
Swan Lake. (We all agreed those swans would be
Hissed off the field at any Southwest half-time show.)
It's not a bad life. No one expects grace or precision.

Outdoors scavenging the city's trash—presents for yourself—
You collect what you can, what you want, what you need.
Last night I found a Lilly Daché hat and three foam mats.
Street life has its dangers: cold, jail, insults.
But no humiliation. A year ago I got knocked up.
Rape, yes, but no mutilation.
It wasn't bad. I don't feel much these days.
I keep the baby, Billielou, in my bag, snug
In a nest of rags, a Dallas kangaroo.
If Beebeelou—that's what I call her—wants
To be a Rangerette . . . Well, I don't know . . .
Her fingers curl around my thumb like little tongues.
She'll have to have her chance to kick her boots to the sky,
To slice it with her legs, the perfect blue
Deep in the heart of Texas.

HOW TO ORDER A FREAK:

Neatly. Precisely. Survey its hump.
Chart its topography. Fathom its veined secrets. See
Following pages for our complete spine of hunchbacks.

Sternly. Boat women require discipline.
They are foul-mouthed and the rooster figureheads
Between their breasts crow doubling curses.
See following pages for our complete list
Of canoe babies, frigate girls and steamship women.

Persuasively. Obsequiously. Dwarfs and midgets,
Some say, top the hierarchy. Our inflatable
Model soars higher than ever. Royal colors:
Scarlet and purple, some ermine-trimmed.
Details on following pages.

Look up. Giants loom. In the warp of their arms
The biggest of us can cradle. See following pages
For a complete line of mothers and fathers.

Carefully. Choose one suited to the task:
The betrayed woman to serve you blowfish
On her platter; the tattooed man to print love on
Your skin; the dog-faced boy
To bring you back to God (see Freak holidays)
And the Thin Man with Spare Muscles, the Murmurmaid,
The Guitar Woman, the Electric Bed and many more.
Each one of a kind, so don't delay.

~

For our complete catalogue,
Send a description of your house
And a full-length photograph of yourself.
Decision of the judges will be final.

THE SECRETS OF E. MUNCH

for Jordan Smith

What showed
In the agonized O of the mouth,
The open arms like knives,
The paint thick as spoiled cream
Was his public secret;
The private one,
Concealed like pubic hair,
Was his love of Grieg,
That other Edvard. Music
Full of girls in white lawn dresses on lupine-studded meadows,
Of blond young men in blue velvet suits, sweetly philandering,
Of suns, fresh as newly hung laundry, rising and rising.
All tensions, the slight pains of D major,
Twinges of A minor, quickly solved in
Tender resolutions.

Grieg pursued him even when he locked
The pianoforte.
Grieg forced him to evident mutilations.
No one would notice as he
Bled through his gloves onto the canvas
That he hummed "The Violet Who Loved the Shepherd."

FLORENCE NIGHTINGALE'S PARTS

Were always straight, straight as her clothes:
The bow on her drawers, symmetrical as a butterfly;
The strings on her corselet like the pattern of a Morris dance;
Her petticoats pleated like a fan, knife sharp;
The buttons on her dress lined in ranks;
The cameo brooch centered at the covered hollow of her neck;
And her part, straight through the waves as if
Moses commanded there. The whole divided as neatly
As the body divides itself by virtue of its pairs.

    I, Florence Nightingale, take these wedded locks
    To have and to hold, to pleat and to fold,
    For richer, for poorer, for better, for worse,
    Lock, stock and barrel.
    War makes more: more money, more disarray.
    Take away the tray, Nellie, I shall eat nothing
    This morning; I am fed up to the teeth.
    O comb, my comb,
    My honey, my hive, but only
    The cocks can stride into battle.
    I am at home without even a wattle.
    For richer, for poorer, for better, for nurse.
    Alone at home with Ma*ma* and Pa*pa*
    And sister, Parthy, my sister,
    Born in Greece like a fever blister.
    Parthenope, Parthenope,
    Watching my comb like a honey bee.
    My comb inlaid with sea foam and mother-of-pearl,
    Parting the waves like the prow of a ship.

A slip of a girl, a drowning, hair
Fanning out in the water
Like flame. Fame is no motive.
Right is. To set things right.
A knight enfolding the world in her black cloak,
Glints off her armor, the stars.
For richer, for poorer.
Crimea fever, Crimea fear.
To have and to hold.
The tableux you planned, a guinea a head,
Will buy supplies sorely needed.
Assigning the princesses the parts
Of the graces should assure the subscription.
My thanks once again.
I am seen as austere. I am not.
Dreams of hair in tight curls,
Unplaited, unbound; first freedom
And lightness, then too light;
They are drawn into my mouth when I breathe.
I drown in my hair.
I am seen as austere. Death comes
From disorder. Partition the cabins.
Boil the sheets. Steer the course for home.
The mate throws the boatswain a Turkish bone.
A bonnet, blue as the vein of the Thames
On the map in the Captain's cabin where I work,
A bonnet will cover the loss of my hair when we land.
Crimea fever, a pox.
Cocks died, the hen did not.

I am spared for my work.
For richer, for poorer;
For better, for worse;
Till death us do part.

Florence Nightingale's parts were
Always straight. She saw to that using the mirror
On the desk which straddled her bed. Red velvet curtains
Hung like wattles from the posts
Between which she commanded:
Sanitation for India, Hospital Reorganization for Birmingham,
Tea for Disraeli.
Her hair grew back, pushing its rivulets
Against the will of her assignment,
But fell out again before she died at ninety,
Fell out completely. Baldness made no difference.
She parted her skin.

A CERTAIN SENSE OF AWE

The hosannas of dwarfs echo, spilling
Liquid from the tree crotch:
Laud, laud, lauda,
Praises ring through the arch of leaves.
This is the other cathedral.
Birds stain the branches
And fill the air with polyphonic color.
The choir of dwarfs moves in misshapen surplices
Cut to fit.
These are ceremonies
Unlisted in *Time* or *The Village Voice,*
Ceremonies where fingers seal themselves
And, like fern fronds uncurling,
Wings appear. Only from too great a distance
Can we see, or only think we see,
Their celebration of what we mourn,
Their slow ascension into a dazzle of light.

A PLACE TO WATCH THE BIRDS

for Michael Fried

The man loves birds but does not
Want to go outside:
Ants get in the food; limbs may
Fall on you in
The wood; it may rain when you are
Far away from buildings.
If you prepare in advance you may sweat
In your slicker or trip
Over your umbrella. Even those beautiful birds
Flickering through the trees,
Their scarlet crests scratching the sky,
Their printed wings writing
On grass may, outdoors, splat droppings on your head.
He builds the birds
An Amusement Park outside his porch—ferris wheel,
Trapezes, convenience food chains—
So he can sit inside and watch them. That way he can keep
An ear cocked
For the phantom baby upstairs who could cry at any moment,
Waking, wanting to be rocked.

IT IS DANGEROUS TO BE THE CONDUCTOR

Then, early on in Act III, he [Sir Georg Solti] stabbed himself in the temple with the point of his third baton. Blood poured down into his right eye, dripping onto the score and music desk.

TIME MAGAZINE, *September 20, 1976*

Lightning does strike twice. Lully thumping the floor with
His staff, beating time for the Paris Opera, beat it to
Death when he hit his foot instead of board:
Gangrene. But beyond the self-inflicted dangers:
What about the second-row cellist with angina pectoris?
The oboist with the wife in Payne Whitney?
And even beyond these, the more familiar:
What about your son who announces he would murder for
Money, who figures prices and vice versa in
The margins of *Ellery Queen's Mystery Magazine?*
What about your daughter who spends
All her time on scrapbooks for orphans,
Combing antique stores for a dessert menu from
The Ritz so she can place *Pêche Melba* next to
The rotogravure diva who, costumed for Tosca,
Is pasted on the page emerging from the pouch of a kangaroo?
As you pound yourself on the foot or stab yourself
In the temple, do you think of Radames suffocating
In the tomb, before he ever had children to settle the score?

WANTED:

for Peter Woolsen

A man in wolf's clothing,
All that thick, seductive hair.
But if it is clothing . . .
The hair can be taken off,
And I will find myself
Part of his harem
As he strides naked
Through the Moorish arches
Across the tiled floor
Toward me. Yet,

If he has none—
Head, beard, pubic—
Perhaps he is the eunuch—
Hairless, testy—guarding
The women whose lusts
Otherwise would break
Out like a disease,
Like Ural Mountain
Spotted Fever.

The cure is upon us:
Knock, knock.
Who's there?

You.
You who?
Eunuch.
"All right; so now
I know who. But
What have you done
With your hair?"

"I left it at the podiatrist
Where I went for my fallen
Arches. Wearing
A wolf suit is hard on the feet."
Our civilization is falling apart:
Effete, hairless men.
And the women growing beards
Bearding the wolf
In his den.
And winning.

THE LADY PITCHER

It is the last of the ninth, two down, bases loaded, seventh
Game of the Series and here she comes, walking
On water,
Promising miracles. What a relief
Pitcher she has been all year.
Will she win it all now or will this be the big bust which
She secures in wire and net beneath her uniform,
Wire and net like a double
Vision version
Of the sandlot homeplate backstop in Indiana where
She became known as Flameball Millie.

She rears back and fires from that cocked pistol, her arm.
Strike one.
Dom, the catcher, gives her the crossed fingers sign,
Air, but she shakes it off and waits for fire.
Strike two.
Then the old familiar cry, "Show them you got balls, Millie."
But she knows you should strike while the iron is hot
Even though the manager has fined her
Sixteen times for disobeying
The hard and fast one:
A ball after two strikes.
She shoots it out so fast
It draws
An orange stripe on that greensward.
Strike three.

~

In the locker room they hoist her up and pour champagne
All over her peach satin, lace-frilled robe.
She feels what she has felt before,
The flame of victory and being loved
Moves through her, but this time
It's the Series and the conflagration matches
The occasion.

In the off-season she dreams of victories and marriage,
Knowing she will have them and probably not it.
Men whisper, in wet moments of passion,
"My little Lowestoft," or, "My curvy Spode," and
They stroke her handle, but she is afraid that yielding means
Being filled with milk and put on
The shelf;
So she closes herself off,
Wisecracking.
When she is alone again she looks at the china skin
Of her body, the crazing, the cracks she put there
To make sure
She couldn't
Hold anything for long.

BEADS IN A RED BOX

for Susan Crile

For all you knew I had left the hospital, gone home. And bled to death on the ticking of a mattress, in a place so unsettled it was without sheets. And they could have brought the winding kind in the ambulance that had been summoned by the woman upstairs when she stopped by to say welcome. And, if you'd finally called, you could have gotten a watchmaker or the child of the family who'd been given my number.

I collect them, these beads, each one
Chosen with as much care as a lover or a friend.
I got the first when I was four, next to the fence
Behind the house on Milton Road, red/pink against
The grass, like a fallen sour cherry. See it,
The coral bead in the middle. Their order is
Their chronology: strung time.
If you look carefully through
The pierced filigree you can see the dog,
Half chow/half collie, whose name was Leila.
Next is one the colors of a Roman silk scarf.
It looks enamel. But experts say
They do not know; I would
Guess, because it was hers,
That rouge and powder
Are a part, or milk and nitrate.

On the other side of center is
The olive stone containing leaves in embryo.
And next to it, grey/white, a bread ball.
Father made them at the table
And gave them to her,
"I will be hurt if you don't
Keep them." The emerald wrapped in
Strands of gold like hair. How perfect
Her circles were on the ice. And her skating
Costume trimmed in fur. But she
Was fair: we alternated as
The heroine and witch.
The shells of striped blister
Beetles are paired, their flat sides
Glued to form the rounded whole. After the fire
We healed, and gradually put our clothes back on.
Paper: the shredded works of Robert Herrick.
Glass: the sea in a bead. A World
War II bullet: it still contains
Its charge of bone.

So different. Yet all the same.
Eat one. Eat ten. They will not
Nourish. Hold up cold hands to them
On a night when the furnace fails.
They will not warm. Put them around

Your neck. They will hang, but not
Embrace. Unrealistic expectations.
As if you'd wished an elephant
An ocean life preserver. A piece of
Wood, an orchestra. If you need
More than ornament, do not choose beads.

*You call and talk of love and give excuses weaker than new
grammar. None is acceptable. Except your own death or
near to that. You are neither/nor. I am adding a bead of
dry ice to the chain.*

THE DANGERS OF LOOKING BACK

for John Unterecker

*Men and women could not share the same table and many
foods were forbidden to the women and common people
under penalty of death.*

ANCIENT HAWAII: *The Volcano Museum*

The volcano has snow on top, concealing
What is beneath
                          Festooned Stalactite of Basalt
Its shield. We drive toward it through
Forests of tree fern.
                          Bearded Stalactite
Volcano Report (dial 543–2121): This week
Little activity; zero chance of quake.
                          Mass of Driblet
Both men my mother married liked
Their toast burned, would
                          Gas Driblet tube
Send it back to the toaster for blackening:
Charcoal, buttered with preserve.
                          Festooned Paho-e-ho-e
We are walking an arrested lava sea, crunching
Waves under foot: they are black, break
With the sound of burnt toast.
Walking like chewing.
                          Fine-grained Vesicular Basalt
In the hotel, Volcano House, after a meal of
Pork with guavas, slathered rice, Asahi Beer
We go to bed and try to lick

Dendritic Aa

The butter off each other until the eruption:
Fountains of fire, red, gold, spurt

        Gypsum needles

Into the air. We run outside, still naked.
Hot ash flakes down like snow

        Pele's hair

And a river of orange lava flows toward us like
Movies of a steel mill. When the lava
Coats us

        Mud raindrops

We are reaching out to each other, not quite
Touching, just as before.

        Epsom Glauber and Alum Salts

CONTAINING

for Marjorie Herrmann

The glass jar stands on the family
Mantel, clearly empty,
As cloudless sky does not reveal
Its currents, its forces.

The woman with the waved hair comes in,
Wearing her purple robe,
And drops in a piece of lapis lazuli,
Then a pom-pom from
The baby's wooly cap, a Mississippi
Clam shard used to irritate
Oysters into pearls, the dead Grandmother's
Autographed Caruso picture,
Square and bow knots made by the Father,
Balls of chocolate walnut fudge,
A handful of potpourri, a gold charm bracelet
Accounting for the events of
The Mother's life, an imitation Dürer etching
Of the Nativity, fireplace ashes,
An albino frog and her own indigestion medicine.

The hurricane has been expelled by its
Replacements. The jar
Stands on the mantel, stuffed; the air
Now only mortar between
Objects. The family is relieved. It has
Avoided something shattering.

REMAINS—STRATIGRAPHY:

for L. D.

must be used with caution, for the altitude at which an object is found does not necessarily determine its stratum. Something that dropped into a well belongs not to the level where it was found at the bottom of the well, but to the level from which it had been dropped.

THE ANCIENT NEAR EAST

1978: Forty-nine inches in New York this year:
Melting, freezing, snow on ice, snow melting,
Freezing into ice, layers covering layers as
The Babylonians covered the Assyrians;
The Assyrians the Chaldeans; the Chaldeans
The Kassites; the Kassites the Amorites;
The Amorites the Sumerians. In the summer
Will we find fragments of the Ishtar Ziggurat
Or thick, brown Manhattan beads?

Ice, a frieze on buildings, forces everything
To stay where it is. Cars rock
Back and forth like women in labor,
Like women in labor needing Caesareans.
Their sound wakes us, interrupts our meals,
Stops our work, makes us bite our nails,
Causes attacks of migraine or colitis.
Some agony touches us even though we know
It is only a Firebird, a Grand Prix, a Lark.
I hold with those who claim someone dies
When tires fight ice.

~

The layers of your letters, sheets stained blue,
Pile into a bed. Endearments, promises, lies
Twist like a wet handkerchief.
1973: You wrote of spring wasps outside your window,
That the fiery nails of their sting . . .
On the Anacassia Savannah Plain
The Carmine Bee Eater rides the Bustard to
Catch bees or locusts which the Bustard's large
Fringed wings comb from the brush. In locust years
Cicadas fall in blizzards on the Bustards.
The Bee Eater rides and eats
Using its carmine beak to warn its mount of danger.

1975: You wrote of the tattooed man,
His skin like paper, water-marked with patterns:
Aphrodite drowning in the vortex of his navel,
Diana wrinkled until passion made her
Spring smooth . . .
On the High Simian Plain
The Gelada baboon flicks its long silky hair
Against flies. It woos by combing hair with its nails,
Picking fleas, licking secretions clean.
Wooing by grooming, the overlord
Turns his pink rump to his harem's chosen one.
You wrote, hear me, believe me:
These letters spell messages as compact and complicated
As a tattoo of passion's fingerprints.

~

1979: Taps.
Music of ice cascades to the pavement.
You write: I hope you are well.
Nails of ice puncture water, merging with it;
A stratum cannot be assigned.
Reflections of stone tattoo the surface.
Whatever the object was,
Nothing remains.

THE LOBSTER

This lobster flown in from Maine to Houston
Lies in a wooden box on cracked ice,
Its green not the green of deep water,
But of decay. Its stalk eyes, which should be
Grains of black caviar, are beads of phlegm.
Through the cracks in its shell, the meat
Shines like oil on water or mother-of-pearl.

I see exactly what it is, yet must wrap it up
In my finest linen handkerchief—the one with
The border and initials pulled by Filipino nuns—
And take it home to keep in my bureau drawer;
So that its smell invades my private places,
And lobster mold begins to form on the edges of fabrics.

I throw open the doors and jalousies, hoping to
Dilute the crustacean air, and you walk in. I had not
Expected to see you again: we had decided.
We inventory everything and redecide: you will stay.
The lobster, smooth and green as deep water, is
Crawling over the blue silk scarf when we
Open the drawer. We cook it for dinner,
In water laved with peppercorns and fennel, and spread
A sheet on the table, anticipating the complete repast.

THE CONCEPTION

Aphrodite Receives a Gift from Hermes

You leave a basket of tomatoes on
My doorstep, succulent as your rounds.
I catch a tip of skin and
Strip the red paper off,
Swallowing the running flesh.
Every mouthful tastes of you.
The red moon juice, sweet
Sharp on my fingers and lips.

When the pains begin, I believe
That old wives' tale:
Love apples: poison.
Pain chews itself into my inside lights,
Beaming spasms through sinuous tissues;
Blood runs mingling with red juice.

The pain organizes itself
And the small purple-red face emerges
Followed by the rest.
Complete, more than complete,
Hermes' gift to Aphrodite.

How Together They Invented a Version
to Conceal What They Knew

The child was growing.
The mushroom velvet of its penis and testes,
The anemone satin of its vulva reminded them

That the child was the implacable record of
What they were together.

Hermes, herald of Zeus,
Hermes, god of eloquence,
Inventor of the lyre, inventor of the syrinx,
The alphabet and numbers,
Charter of star paths and resolutions
Of modes, Phrygian, Mixolydian.
Hermes, master of the headlock,
Instructor on the cultivation of olive trees.
Hermes, god of luck who squares the dice,
God of sacrifices who tends the goats, the rams,
Saves them for the slaughter,
Protects them for the sacrifice,
Place around Hermaphroditus
Your sacred objects:
Palm trees, four tortoises, one each
Blowfish, spiny grout,
Silver eel, halibut.
Hide the child behind a twine of fronds
And shells and fish;
Then with Aphrodite invent the tale
Of a young man and a fountain nymph
Who loved him so she prayed to join with him;
Write it on ewes' skin, thin as the peel of love apples;
So that all will believe he was as she was
Because of love not vengeance.

THE MOSAIC HUNCHBACK

In the Hanging Gardens at Graz stands Grosswunch,
The Mosaic Hunchback, a twelve-foot marvel designed by
The visionary architect, Moses Wurmtaffel in 1520,
Executed, but never killed, by generations of Grazers,
Bit by bit. Part parti-colored completion, part empty
Filigree, each orifice—space defined by stopped space—
Accepted and accepts its new propitiation, bite by bite.

> The women say, "We have a Guild, the gold
> Sign in the shape of a pregnant belly hangs
> Outside the hall where we meet."
>   Join us, join us.

As in the old tales of competition for the hand of
The maiden, marriages cannot be consummated until
The suitor finds his assigned piece—a shard of flesh-red
Feldspar from Peking, the tip of an orange goose-beak
From Hanover, a sliver of silver Electra wing from Seattle—
And has sealed it into its hole, its wet grout mouth.

> Each week on Monday the women meet
> To exchange words: faceted or rubbery or
> Covered with blood; words: quietly, softly
> From mouth to ear. We hear what we hear.
>   Join us, join us.

~

Der Grosse Moses had set the task of keeping
The spirit alive to the whole town, piece by piece.
Men, it is said, do their part in action—the search—
And humped affirmation: "Peace in our town;
Embroider that on our festival banners," they order.

> They say women have only their tears—
> Running freely as salt, the cellar's
> Mosaic bit, or water, its release—
> And their parts which the men believe
> They assign. But we know they do not.
> > Join us, join us.

The Hunchback had only one eye from 1810 until last week.
Now the shoemaker's son has put in the second—
The wood knot of a Blue Beech tree he went to Poland Springs
To find. Defined now, and defining, he claims his pride,
His bride, and smiles as they play *Lohengrin,* reminding her
In spite of her beseeching, there can be no questions.

> Some women warn, "There are rules and rulers
> As sharply delineated as the side of one or
> The slide." Others say, "They wear clothes,
> But we see them naked, see their mosaic skin."
> "We, too, can have patterned flesh," say three,
> Standing on a Super Giant box of All. Some wring
> Their hands trying to decide; some know.
> > Join us, join us.

~

The Hunchback presides over the town's brocade ceremonies,
Looking on now with both eyes. It is said that two
Unmentionable holes must remain open; so that each Spring
The newly hatched maggots may pour out: to clean
The town's flesh, to leave the bones of the town polished,
To signify that the Holy Ghost resides where He will.

> Each week on Moonday, the women meet.
> The shoemaker's son's wife comes, holding
> Her baby whose skin is as soft as
> Lamb's-wool socks. The three women want
> To pick holes in it to form a mosaic baby.
> We expel them with plain skin and lullabies.
>   Join us, join us.

When the holes run out, will they make a bride for him?
The mosaic Hunchbreast? Will the Hunchback design her or
Have designs on her? No one knows. The mosaic egg could be
Halfway around the world or it could contain the universe.
Blood myths are as hard to hold as blood. They cannot be read.

> Join us, join us.

II

BURYING THE BABIES

for Barbara Kellerman

*Common
School
Classics,
1846*

"Does this book tell all about such pretty things, mother?"
said Charles, going up to the table and turning the leaves.
"What is that man looking into the round box for, mother?
—Is he sitting on a table?"

*Leonardo
da Vinci,
letter, 1482*

If occasion should arise, I can construct cannon and mortars
and light ordnance in shape both ornamental and useful and
different from those in common use.

*What
a Woman
of 45
Ought to
Know,
Dr. Emma
Drake,
1902*

Sit down, dear sisters, and candidly question yourselves. Are
you doing right when you lay down your arms, after the
careful drilling of the years behind you and say there is
nothing more for you to do or dare? . . . How suffering
humanity is crying for the helpfulness of home-gendered
virtues. How motherless men and women are fainting for
the comforting which blessed women, who have filled and
beautified the home with practical womanliness, can alone
give them. O homekeepers tread softly!

*The
Puppet
Theater
of Japan,
A. C.
Scott*

Female puppets have neither feet nor legs. The junior pup-
peteer simulates their appearance by placing both hands be-
neath the kimono and gripping the inner hem with the
thumb and forefinger of the left hand and the forefinger
and middle finger of the right hand. It sounds a compara-
tively simple operation, but it requires infinite skill and
understanding to do it properly. In its way it is just as im-
portant as the more spectacular manipulation of the head.

Sources for the quoted material may be found following this poem.

49

If I give you water in my right hand, will you
Be able to hold onto it? I have been trained for forty-five years
To hold on: to stand on my head on a ladder; to prize litter
Until there is no room for me in the room; to letter
Signs in Gold Gothic; to let: sentences escape because
They are not supposed to blot, and flushings clog because it
Is too expensive to call the plumber or the beautician;
To let: soup spoil because we might need it for tomorrow's
Picnic; to let: a bed-sitter for two pounds a week,
The contribution of Weight Watchers, who are sponsoring
The Strong Man Contest at the Washington County Fair.
He begins with the lift and jerk and becomes the latter
When he heaves up that three-hundred-and-fifty-pound woman,
Vomits her all over the crowd; so that they are picking
Kidneys, fingers, all her parts out of their flower-trimmed
Straw hats, their beards, their all-day suckers for weeks.

If I give you water in my right hand will it repress fingers?

Love
and Will,
Rollo May

The old Puritans repressed sex and were passionate; our new
puritan represses passion and is sexual. . . . I define this
puritanism as consisting of three elements. First, *a state of
alienation from the body.* Second, *the separation of emotion
from reason.* And third, *the use of the body as a machine.*

To wait on my head on a ladder for the winner of the Strong Man
        Contest,
The Atlas Contest at the Washington County Fair.

Puppet
Theater

When a male puppet steps forward he places his left foot first, the female puppet, her right foot. This is the differentiation between the sexes.

When a puppet calls out another's name it points at the skies with its hand.

Heaves up that three-hundred-and-fifty-pound woman, a new Constellation, claiming the sky with her parts.

The
Pleasures
of Hope,
Thomas
Campbell,
1861

At summer eve, when Heav'n's aerial bow
Spans with bright arch the glittering hills below,
Why to yon mountain turns the musing eye,
Whose sunbright summit mingles with the sky?
Why do those cliffs of shadowy tint appear
More sweet than all the landscape smiling near? —
'Tis distance lends enchantment to the view,
And robes the mountains in its azure hue.

But on the whole this Fair is truly that:
Fair, fair, my love, trimmed with caracul, white cumulus,
The red-and-white striped tents glued on blue sky;
So that during the Star Spangled, the crowd can look at any
Horizon and feel tricolored blood pulsing reflexively.
And we can kiss before you are called away by
Your service. When I was a child and heard
FDR on the radio, I always stood for our anthem, my eyes
Circling the room to find a red pincushion, white paper,
Blue cornflowers. Blue cornflower: bachelor's button. The groom

Plucks it out of his lapel, as he walks away
From the altar after the ceremony, to indicate he
Is no longer one. (Is that a sentence?) Then he goes out to care for
The horses because matrimony doesn't mean a day off from
The job: "The horses must be curried every day."

*How
to Write,
Gertrude
Stein,
1931*

A sentence made by coupling meanwhile
a couple there makes grateful dubeity
named atlas coin in a loan . . .
Sentences may be alike.
Harbour this for me.
She harbours this for me.
Sentences make use of waning.

The moon wanes into adolescence, a stage. Our eyes
Circle the room for its parts, diagraming, parsing.

*Common
School
Classics*

No, my dear, it is a platform, or stage, to hold that large
box as you call it. The box is a telescope through which that
gentleman is looking at the beautiful moon. He can see it
almost as plain as you can see your face in a mirror, and
that book tells what he sees.

You hold the moon, a grapefruit, above your head
As your wife reads the sentence and I
Wait with water in my right hand.

Ten o'clock was the luncheon hour, when all the family met,
and my Great-Aunt Louisa was always much in evidence.

Louisa
of Tuscany,
Ex-Crown
Princess,
1911

She was a dwarf, with the crooked malicious mind that so
often goes with a crooked body. She had very long, monkey-
like arms and whenever she was displeased she would fling
them out like the sails of a windmill and hit whichever of
her ladies-in-waiting happened to be nearest her.

After the ceremony, the groom demonstrates his prowess
By holding everything up, as the ladies-in-waiting wait.

Louisa
of Tuscany

At eight came the *dîner de cérémonie,* which the children
heartily enjoyed, as they had had no food since ten o'clock
in the morning and my father has often told me how raven-
ously hungry they used to become.

"Yes, it's delicious though fiery."
"Oh, use the condiments: the coconut, the banana, the nuts,
The raisins, the chutney to tamp the flame in your mouth."
"It tastes like beef, but I know the cooks are Hindus."
"Perhaps it is buffalo, perhaps horse. Curry covers
The exacter flavors."
"My mouth is still on fire."
"Here, take this water in my hand."
"Your hand is empty . . . Excuse me, I must make
A phone call: check with my service."
I am afraid he will never see, even as
The waves wash over his fingers, the white foam, like
The ruching of his wife's wedding dress, tickles

The hair on his knuckles. He denies the water
As I say, "Drink." Denies what the hand harbors.
Yes, there is salt in it and you cannot tell before
You swallow if it will bite the tongue, delighting as it
Sustains. Or will leave you dead in the drifting lifeboat.
With no one to take care of the babies.

*Reasons
for
Moving,
Mark
Strand*
    Let us hurry
    Let us save the babies.

The waves wash over his ankles: the foam,
Like the lace on my nightgown, tickles his legs.

*Soils,
S. W.
Fletcher,
1907*
    The minute root hairs are always absorbing water, together
with the plant food that is dissolved in it; not free water,
but the film water clinging to the grains of soil.

He reads me the symptoms of thirst but refuses
To drink, "Turn on 'The Late Show.' " Film water. Movie salt.

*Lifeboat,
Twentieth
Century-Fox,
1944*
    Hume Cronyn, at the tiller, to John Hodiak, as Tallulah
Bankhead looks angrily at Hodiak: "Neither can a snake
help being born a snake instead of a nightingale. A German
can't help being born a German."

"Tallulah had that hoarse voice anyway. It had nothing to do
With the sinking. Or did it? She never mentioned curry."
"No, the writers at Fox never did. They wrote the dialogue.
She delivered it."
We are floating in my bed, a safe berth we hope,
Watching them struggle with their oars.
They are up to their ears in vines.
"Malaya? Brian Donlevy?"
"No, Alabama. Bette Davis. Tallulah played it
On Broadway. Bankhead, a better last name for *The Little Foxes.*"
She got all the money. Murder covered by
Batting her eyelashes. Magnolia. Honeysuckle.
That's the Southern way of suckling.
I must go to the nursery to check the babies.
They are safe behind glass.

*Louisa
of Tuscany*

Queen Caroline seems to have possessed considerable indi-
viduality, and she must have been a woman of exceptional
courage and iron constitution for she insisted on accom-
panying her husband to the Napoleonic wars, and rode by
his side, indifferent to discomfort and fatigue. She had
sixteen children and nursed them all herself; the youngest
infant went through these campaigns with her, in charge of
a nurse, and the Queen used to dismount at intervals and
suckle her baby, sitting by the roadside.

That's the Southern way of suckling. What's the
Southern way of suckling? All-day suckers.

What's red and white on the outside and grey and white on the inside? Campbell's Cream of Elephant Soup.

Soup. Curlicued lintels. Do I mean lentils? Soup.
Sole. I am cooking, garnishing with parsley,
Currying favor, flavoring filet of sole for you.

The window washer leaves the prints of his neoprene Cats Paw #6
Soles on the radiator. Then he leaves the window,
Falling when a loop gives way. The water stays in his hand
As the law of falling bodies says it will.

C.M.   My Dear, As I look at your lighted window across the park,
I look through dirty glass because the window washer never
came. I know you won't like it when I agree with Richard
and say, Labor is so impossible these days . . .

They have given up high forceps; so they no longer grab
The duodenum by mistake instead of the baby.
In this case, there are two, but not twins: sisters.
Clearly not twins: one weighs three pounds,
Has no fingernails and eyes with a film of soup over them;
The other weighs twelve and is developed in all her particulars:
There is definitely several months separating them.
The Spaniards will be absolutely fascinated with **this**;
They are so fond of oddities, they may rename a square
In Seville as they did with the three-headed swallow.

A sentence divided into three.
There are these in dissatisfac-
tion. One must make three be-
How · fore them seldom as chance.
to Write · Never allowed to wait. A sen-
tence divided into three. He is
never to be allowed to continue
to commence to prepare to wait.

I am waiting because the window washer never came. Babies
Are so impossible these days.

Tears may be wiped away with the left hand once in every
Puppet · three times, but if the puppet has its back turned to the
Theater · audience, the left hand may only be used once during the
course of the play.

In my left hand I give you notes: Purcell, Schubert; for
Stanzas; due and overdue. One minute the notes
Look like emeralds. Then like drops of water on blue-notched
Petals. Then like air. Airs: on a flute, a trombone.
Rounds. Canons. Royal Fireworks Music. I wonder if you
Will be able to hold music in your hand. You want to, but
You weigh everything so carefully, even scales.

~

Notes due and overdue:

	Du meine Seele, Du mein Herz;
"Widmung,"	Du meine Wonne, O, du, mein Schmerz;
R. Schumann/	Du mein Welt darein ich lebe;
F. Rückert,	Mein Himmel, du, darein ich schwebe;
1840	Mein gutter Geist, mein bessres Ich.

On the polished brass scales, their rounds like suns,
It took weeks for you to measure, to assay, to say
We could meet for lunch. And then there wasn't any.
It was a vegetarian restaurant. The lentils with
Chopped parsley matched your eyes as you spread the mixture
On the Chapati. There were red swallows and Missions on
The wallpaper. A tryst. Even though you had taken off
Your ring and put a cornflower in your lapel, I watched
Your hands and knew there were still problems.

	Born—Bridalled—Shrouded—
"Title	In a day—
Divine—	Tri Victory
Is Mine,"	"My husband"—women say—
Emily	Stroking the Melody—
Dickinson	Is *this*—the way?

You weigh everything so carefully, on the polished brass
Scales, their rounds like glistered snails.

But I was not naughty or cross; I was trying to pull this
great worm out of this pretty shell; I am better than a worm
and I want it myself. I shook the ugly thing and pulled him,
but see how he crawls in again on purpose to tease me.

In your fist you hold what we will become: the game: shells.
The game: paper, rock, scissors. The game: cards.
Carmen's fortune: Spades: "Toujours la mort."

The old woman in the lavender robe, which fades like afternoon
     light,
Sits playing solitaire in the window framed by the curlicued
Lintels, framed by concrete garlands. ("Framed, I was framed,"
John Garfield leaned against the door, leaking blood and
Words at his blonde girl who looked like the angel on
Top of a Christmas tree. "Baby, I love you," and most
Of the women, even the ones who'd won china, sighed, thinking
Of their own husbands who'd never drag themselves, bleeding,
Through Hell's Kitchen to die speaking of love. THE END: the
     women
Clapped as the music of the electric organ played them out.)
She is drinking from a cup she got at Loew's in '34
As she sits at the table, sorting earrings, cards, stockings, Victrola
Records, trying to make pairs out of her accumulation, a match
For herself. She does. And it catches the hem of the sleeve of
Her lavender robe. And in a second she is all flame,
Sitting Suttee. "Toujours la mort." Only immediate water could
Save her, but the nearest is in the hand of the falling
Window washer. "What a Chanukah candle!" says a child across
     the street.

Ah, ah, ah . . . ah, ah.

Lakmé,
Léo Delibes,
1883

Ah, ah, ah . . . ah, ah.

Lakmé's cadenza, above the Hindoo chorus, from the aria, "Where Goes the Maiden Straying?" or, "The Bell Song"

Louisa
of Tuscany

The opera is always associated in my mind with an incident which I shall describe as the "Affair of the *Collier*." As everyone knows, the Emeralds of the King of Saxony have world-wide reputation, and when I was married they were given to me to wear set in a tiara, necklace and bracelet. I was delighted to possess the wonderful setting so I asked and received permission to have the necklace made smaller.

The light from the candle refracts through the emeralds. You have
Upset them; they lie in a heap beyond the pail, on the sill.

Louisa
of Tuscany

The beauty of the stones, and my own sense of the artistic, resulted in my ordering an entirely new *collier* in a lovely Renaissance design. I decided to wear it at a gala performance, and chose a delightful rose chiffon gown to act as a foil to its mysterious green splendour; and it was with conscious pride in my appearance that I seated myself in my box opposite to the King and Queen who were on the other side of the Opera House.

The flaws of emeralds concealed by lapidary skill.
Perfected in the Jewish quarter of Amsterdam, transported
By the Spanish invaders to Seville, along with the clap.

Directly they saw me, they stared, and stared again, with opera-glasses leveled at my *collier*. A whispered consultation took place, and I was summoned to the royal box. The King received me very coldly and asked me how I *dared* alter the family heirlooms.

I have a fever. You come into my bedroom carrying your
Black bag, "I never care for members of my own family."
"I know; but you do for me."
Seal me up; sew me up.
Button my lip; close my cup.
Leave me alone till I grow cold.
Let no pencil pierce that fold,
That sheet, that skim of skin;
Nothing, no one will I allow in.
As Saran Wrap keeps the food in the bowl,
As the bag of membrane encases the foal,
As clenched teeth keep the tongue within,
So now will this, my virgin skin
Renewed, stretched taut by the surgeon's art:
Hymen's protection; Bonaparte.

"What happened to my baby?" [to Walter Slezak, the German] "You killed him, didn't you? He's in the sea, so big and terrible."

Sew the baby's shroud around her.
Reserve the box for the King and Queen.

Things,
1954

With Napoleon are associated the exploration of interior lines and central positions, economy in force by massing superior strength at the vital point; pinning down the enemy with a strategic advanced guard while manoevering with the rest of the army; preparing the attack by heavy artillery bombardments; and making decisive use of a powerful reserve kept intact during the earlier phase of a battle of attrition.

You come into my bedroom, carrying pastries, loops of custard
And caramel, serving my greed. I may die of consumption.

Common
School
Classics

"Don't hurt that harmless little creature, Frederick: put it on the grass: don't pull so; it is cruel," said Anna to her brother, an interesting little boy about five years old.

It is beginning to rain at the Fair. Water falls from those
Curly clouds, now grey caracul. How fortunate I checked
The babies in the coatroom. Even though I am afraid I may
Mislay the stubs. We carefully wrap the pressed lamb sandwiches,
The Russian pork, the petits fours, and lettuce, lettuce,
Closing the wicker hamper. Water has failed; I have begun
To try food. A few people in the crowd are smoking
And we wonder if the rain has saved them from catching.
You smoke; I do not. The rain is changing to sleet,
Out of the linen closet, glazing the tents and ground,
Coating the sidewalks. Pigeons on the glass, alas, slide.
Only parsley still grows in the borders which, like

Rooming houses, separate Fair town from city. Parsley
Survives the ice; I pick it as emblem, weave it into garlands
And gird you. Parsley green fire. Bright illumination.
Green curls twining with yours, green in brown hair.

Soils

One of the most efficient and certainly the most notorious
of the soil binders is "quack grass" and its counterparts vari-
ously known as "Johnson grass," "witch grass," "couch
grass" and other aliases. The evil reputation of this grass
is due to the fact that it is extremely difficult to kill, because
the long underground pieces may root at any point. The
smaller the pieces into which the roots are chopped by the
irate husbandman, the more widely and thoroughly the pest
is scattered.

How fortunate I checked the babies in the coatroom.
The spade. Their hands. Their feet.

Puppet
Theater

To walk softly, the body should be bent and the things
lifted; to walk in darkness, the hands are extended.

In my three rooms, three clauses, three closets, there is
A constant choice: the field, the sea, the blood.
They keep moving; move me: into the yard where
I measure the acreage of a field, blood flowers in
Its green waves; into the Red Sea which I cook,
Stirring it, seasoning to intensify the smell of mimosa;
Into blood which pulses with sea songs and closes

Its arteries in the season of lust. Do not forget
These are choices, I say to myself, watching the blood
Lap at the wicker cradles. Trim the wick if you want
The kerosene chair to work, if you want the execution
To be perfect. I look for the sentence
In the places I might have left it: the field, the sea,
The blood. But I cannot remember where. Nothing is distinct.
I must question the babies, looking into their grave faces.

Dictionary   Mare Fecunditatis, a dark plain in the fourth quadrant and
extending into the first quadrant of the face of the moon
. . . Also called Sea of Fertility, Sea of Plenty.

I chose the field, thick with daisies and Queen Anne's lace
And mines. Mines which may be full of emeralds.

Lives
of a Cell,
Lewis
Thomas   Almost anything that an animal can employ to make a sound
is put to use. Drumming, created by beating the feet, is used
by prairie hens, rabbits, and mice; the head is banged by
woodpeckers and certain other birds; the males of death-
watch beetles make a rapid ticking sound by percussion of
a protuberance of the abdomen against the ground . . .

It is time for a resting place, a place of nothing.
We are worn out, like screws turned overtime: we, you, I,
They, he, she are all worn out. But no place is nothing.
Even a platform is board. And right there you have one of
The greatest fears. Next to loneliness, singleness. Not

Singularity. That we wear proudly like a ruff of beard or
A red straw hat. You see *things* creep back in
(Snails into their houses). And around the platform,
Concrete now to avoid being board,
There should also be something. If it is sky we are forced
To deal with surrealism, and life is difficult enough without
Clouds as part of the art deco. Walls would be more comfortable
Because we are used to realism. But how can we cut out
Windows and doors, when we don't want them or when we do,
With a disjoined pair of scissors. That tiny screw
Wore out in 1934. We turn to our *Guide to Resting Places*
And find it tells us a platform has so many stories.
That won't do.
We turn to our map of Spas and find the watering holes
Are being used by the horses. They've been exhausted
And won't do.
We turn to the sextant and are told it will not give
Direction today, but we use it anyway because the moon
Has been violated and the sun is too excessive for a time
Afraid of emotion.
Only the constellations
May do. If we approach without gravity. Without weight.

What   I wish it were incumbent upon us, as with the Jews, to enjoy
a Woman   a week in booths and tents at least once a year. Take off to
of 45   the woodlot on your farm, or to the nearest place of the
Ought to   kind you can reach.
Know

We turn to our *Guide to Resting Places*.
It directs us to the bull ring at Mysore.

So much the better (worse)	Tanto mejor (peor)
Thank goodness!	¡Menos mal!
What a nuisance!	¡Que fastido!
What a bore!	¡Que aburrido!
How awful!	¡Que barbaridad!
It doesn't matter.	No importa.
What's on?	¿Que echan?
He is reliable.	Es muy formal.
He has the cheek of a devil.	Es una cara dura.
My goodness!	¡Dios mio!

How to get rid of a bull in the herb garden:
Grab the brass ring in his nose. Use a spade to dig up the herbs.
How to get rid of stains on your doilies:
Pick a shade darker than the darkest stain and dye them.

How to get rid of a whorehouse in your building:
Call the block captain. Ask him to put aside his *Legos*
To investigate. Yes. The place was listed in *Screw*.
He will call the landlord. No. The tenant is a lawyer, not
A pimp. He moved in Xerox machines and calculators.
No offense. Next, the police. They can do nothing unless
A customer will press charges. But the customers are too busy
Screwing on the Xerox machines to undertake laundry.
Everything is ironclad. Get mothers with babies, and
Old ladies in wheelchairs to picket. A picket fence.

A rapier. Insufficient. Release the rats kept in
The basement. The chase will empty the house of its spayed
Cats. Now you have learned to get rid of pimples, look
Carefully at the Air Force. A more difficult target,
Alas. When they bombed Harlem, they said
They thought it was the Nevada Proving Ground.

Motto
of the   Sustineo alas (Lat.)—I sustain the wings.
U.S. Air
Force

"Scalpel." You are incising a baby. It was born
With double shoulder blades, like wings.

                  When it is impossible to use cannon I can supply in their
Leonardo   stead catapults, mangonels, *trabocchi,* and other instruments
da Vinci,   of admirable efficiency not in general use—in short, as the
letter   occasion requires I can supply infinite means of attack and
                  defense.

Each morning, my parsley glued in his curly brown hair,
He dons his robes of office and goes there.
Boxed in by the formal walls he takes out his box of cures:
Hams, tobacco, herring, and decides which patients will get what.
Slice, roll, shred; slice, roll, shred: he makes his preparations.
Or plans his battles, mapping lines of strategy on their scalps, their
        stomachs,
Their breasts/chests. Where will the armies engage

On these hills of flesh? He consults his engagement book
But throws it in the basket when all it yields is a list of fiancées.
He consults the gardening manual, but its pages are full of parsley
And the office is already overgrown: walls, ceiling, carpet
Flocked with parsley.

Tennyson,
1869
Flower in the crannied wall,
I pluck you out of the crannies,
I hold you here, root and all, in my hand,
Little flower—but *if* I could understand
What you are, root and all, and all in all,
I should know what God and man is.

Boxed in by the formal walls,
He reads his book on cells.

School
Composition,
Scott
Macdonald
Ms. Wharton states his heart was jerking between two ex-
tremes of feeling. I think she is implying that his obligatory
sense is being pulled two different ways. Unfortunately Ethan
is not a strong man in will. His loyalty to Zeena and her
damn sickness is stronger than his loyalty to himself. Zeena
is not the one to succumb to her complications; Ethan is.

Parsley seeding, multiplying.
This place will soon be a jungle of green.
He has looked for relief everywhere: Welfare, *bas,*
A young Erikson. There is none here; only escape into

The box within the box, closing the lid: his wife making dinner, his son
Shooting baskets, using an air rifle, his daughter, who notices,
Wondering, when he sits in the Barcalounger listening to
Bach, where he goes. Outside the box
Into the blood's magnetic field, the mine field where
The sky is emblazoned with fireworks bursting in air.
He wears his red biretta, emblazoned with parsley, as
He lectures on cardinal ordinance. Counting down:
Three, two, one. Outside the box. The mine field. Mine.

Puppet
Theater
A general looks back when he stands up; other puppets look
back only when they leave the stage.

Time
Magazine
Two elegantly slim silver-gilt angels hold up a casket sur-
rounded by a crown, studded with rubies and emeralds. It
is traditionally believed to contain the only relic left on earth
by Jesus Christ. True, Christ ascended bodily into Heaven
before the eyes of the astonished Apostles after his resur-
rection. But he had been circumcised in the temple as an
infant and the Holy Foreskin, preserved by a succession of
devout guardians, is said to have found its way eventually
into the sanctum sanctorum of the Vatican.

In the museum they are having an exhibition of the oceans.
Each floor contains its own and the wings contain
Seas, rising and falling like gulls, like our bodies.
The children at the shore of the Aegean
Run naked, stuffing myths into their pails:
A woman is born a mermaid so her husband knows

She cannot run away once he lands her.
A woman is born a mermaid so she can swim,
Carrying plates of water vegetables and fish
To her father who stretches under a red-and-white-striped
Umbrella at the beach. A woman is born a mermaid
So that she will win only sack races,
And, once in a while, the egg and spoon.
A woman is born a mermaid so there will always be
Scales available for weighing flour and justice.
The mothers at the Aegean tend their children,
Stroking their bare bodies, admiring the contents
Of their pails. And the sun shines on them like brass.
It is the same on the floor containing the Antarctic
Except that it is dark and the waves have claws of
Ice, and the mermaids are part seal and the men part bear.
In the lobby, water laps at the marble pillars.
The sea is lapis lazuli. The tenants from the fifth floor
Are visiting the downstairs, sitting by the warm shore,
Holding their children in their laps.

In the museum, they are having an exhibition of the babies.
Their wings rise and fall with each breath.

ANGEL FOOD AND SUNSHINE CAKES

The Gold Cook Book, Louis P. DeGouy, 1947

DEFECT: *Cakes Fall When In or Out of Oven*

1. Oven too hot.
   Reduce temperature accordingly.
2. Egg whites whipped too much.
   Reduce whipping time. Do not whip whites dry.

3. Too much liquid.
   Do not add water to mixture.
4. Improperly cooled.
   Invert cakes in pans on rack to cool.
5. Contamination.
   Check storage room for sources of contamination.

It is too cool to swim; so the children make beads out of
Lapis lazuli, polishing the water with sand.

We are lying on sand at the beach, alone under a discus sun.
The Vs of our legs, seen from above, would make W.
Your face seen from above, your open mouth.
My tongue. Your mouth sucking, swallowing.
The fugue of seagull cries drops guilt, blinding as a halo,
Between us. We are no longer gullible and should know better.
The sky coalesces into sunset and ignites.
When the sea catches your eye, a tear of fire forms
And spills into my hand where I hold it.
Waves, cymbals, crash appropriately.

*"The
Forsaken
Merman,"
Matthew
Arnold,
1849*   . . . There dwells a lov'd one,
        But cruel is she.
        She left lonely for ever
        The kings of the sea.

A woman is born a mermaid so she can picket
For the rights of both women and fish.

"Let your moderation be known to all," would be an excellent motto for women at forty-five and thereabouts. Be quiet and patient and, as a rule, all will be well.

Waves, cymbals, clash appropriately.

She is changed.
Ring the changes. Ring the bells.
They peal, their round brass mouths
Tonguing the news. It is delicious
As grapefruit, as the bite of salt oranges.
She sits in a crewel chair in her waiting dress,
Green with appliqués of iridescent turquoise,
Painting her eyes to match. Out of habit
She bats her lashes at him. Home run.
And in the belfry the bells cook the music of Martin Luther
As black shapes fly out like alphabets.
She knows she should check the babies. But she is
A lady-in-waiting. The bells rent the air.
Families rent apartments and open windows to
Expel the scent of citrus which hangs in the air
Like coal gas. An incendiary woman
Could sing a torch song and light up the city.

The word is out that the sky is not limitless; it is finite. It is, in truth, only a kind of local roof, a membrane under which we live, luminous but confusingly refractile when suffused with sunlight. We can sense its concave surface a

few miles above our heads. We know that it is tough and
thick enough so that when hard objects strike it from out-
side they burst into flame.

Ring the changes; let the clappers
Tongue the air until they flame.

<table>
<tr><td>How
to Write</td><td>If we do a widow sees an old story with new eyes he does
what they do. It is a movement with a in between. What is
a. A dog a call a having this or that. This may be as their
sentence. A reapproach.</td></tr>
</table>

She sits in a crewel chair in her waiting dress
Cross-stitching "toujours l'amour" on a sampler.

<table>
<tr><td>Common
School
Classics</td><td>"Cruel, Anna," said he, looking in her face with a queer
and thoughtful expression—"cruel, cruel, Aunt Patty told
me that pretty chair in her parlor was worked all over with
cruel. Do you think I should be like the picture, or the
chair, or what?"</td></tr>
</table>

They are serving the jugged hares on the holly-rimmed platter
At Christmas dinner. In the middle of the arguments
Which are shaking the silvered globes, Aunt Jean says,
"It's all relative." Yes, Father, Sister, Uncle, Mother,
Great Aunt, Cousin, Grandma, Brother. (Do two syllables signify
Opposition?) I am walking around the table, waiting,
With a handful of water and a handful of dressing:

Himself, myself, yourself, herself (two).
Self, self, put it on the shelf (one). That's the only way
To survive these Christmas courses. And yet I couldn't
Stay away completely, pining, playing Solitaire at
The window on this day of expectation, sharp as
The prick of fresh needles on the tree.
I must go to the playpens to check the babies.

*How
to Write*

Why is an hour glass what they knew was a treasure as they
went without their wanted as they knew as a tree at Christ-
mas. It is a sentence as first to last that they had it in their
out of their however power. They will not give it their per-
mission.

The babies are all right. Pretending to write.
What else to do with a play pen?
Each is alone, rapt, except for the near-twins
Who are sibyls, able to tell what will hold
Water by stirring the cauldron. Syllables swim up
Through the salt broth, defining the rest if we could
Understand them. I return to the dining room; they are serving
The *Lutefisk,* lye-soaked Christmas cod.

*What
a Woman
of 45
Ought to
Know*

Get away from home as often as you can, it will do the
family good to miss you, and they had better far be without
you for a week or two occasionally, than to miss you for all
time. Many a mother would be spared to her family were
she to heed such advice as this and not go drudging along
until tired nature demands the rest that never ends. Never

mind what social functions are demanding your time; get away from them all; it is your duty, the other is not. Duties never conflict.

I couldn't stay away completely. Pining.
Ailing. Waiting for the bier.

"The   All the great things of life are swiftly done,
Widow   Creation, death and love, the double gate.
in the Bye   However much we dawdle in the sun
Street,"   We have to hurry at the touch of Fate;
John   When Life knocks at the door no one can wait.
Masefield,   When Death makes his arrest we have to go.
1912

They are serving the Christmas cod in the dying room
As the vats of dye bubble emerald, parsley green,
Lapis lazuli, citrus yellow, red, white and blue.

                  Midnight came: the fireworks did not succeed, they were
                  covered with a thick cloud; they cost sixteen thousand francs.
Mme.   At four o'clock in the morning Vatel went round and found
de Sévigné,   everybody asleep. He met one of the underpurveyors, who
letter,   had just come in with only two loads of fish. "What!" said
1671   he, "is this all?" "Yes, sir," said the man, not knowing that
                  Vatel had dispatched other people to all the seaports around.

                  Vatel waited for some time; the other purveyors did not ar-
                  rive; his head grew distracted; he thought there was no

more fish to be had. He flew to Gourville: "Sir," said he, "I cannot outlive this disgrace." Gourville laughed at him. Vatel, however, went to his apartment, and setting the hilt of his sword against the door, after two ineffectual attempts, succeeded in the third, in forcing the sword through his heart.

We are resting, arresting probabilities.
We have stopped eating because the food burns our mouths.
We have stopped drinking because we cannot hold the water
In our hands. We have stopped dressing because
Our clothes may catch fire, may attract it, trap it,
The way a tree draws lightning. Dark, the room
Is getting dark, begetting it. We lie in bed and are not
Much more truthful out of it. We reach for each other
Even though we are losing our skin. Scurvy and
Dehydration, I guess. The holding on is
Painful, as the air is painful, and I do not think
I can let go. It is time
To look at the boxes. To check the babies.

Angell's Union Series of Common School Classics, Stereotype Edition. E. H. Butler and Company, Philadelphia, 1846.

Arnold, Matthew. "The Forsaken Merman." 1849.

Blake, Robert, ed. *101 Elephant Jokes*. Pyramid Publishers, New York, 1964.

Campbell, Thomas. "The Pleasures of Hope." Sampson Low Son and Company, London, 1861.

Collins Phrase Books: Spanish. William Collins Sons and Company Ltd., London and Glasgow.

da Vinci, Leonardo. Letter to the Duke of Milan, 1482.

DeGouy, Louis P. *The Gold Cook Book*. Greenberg Publisher, New York, 1947.

Delibes, Léo. *Lakmé*, An Opera. 1883.

Dickinson, Emily. "Title Divine Is Mine," *The Poems of Emily Dickinson*. Martha Dickinson Bianchi and Alfred Leete Hampson, eds. Little, Brown and Company, Boston, 1944.

Drake, Emma F. Angell, M.D. *What a Woman of Forty-Five Ought to Know: Purity and Truth*. Self and Sex Series. Vir Publishing Company, Philadelphia, 1902.

Fletcher, S. W. *Soils*. Doubleday, Page and Company, Garden City, New York, 1907.

Gibb-Smith, Charles Harvard, and Grigson, Geoffrey eds. *Things: A Volume About the Origin and Early History of Many Things, Common and Less Common, Essential and*

Inessential, Limited Edition. People, Places, Things, and Ideas Series. The Waverly Book Company, London, 1954.

Hitchcock, Alfred, director. *Lifeboat.* A film by Twentieth Century-Fox, 1944.

Louisa of Tuscany, Ex-Crown Princess of Tuscany. *My Own Story.* G. P. Putnam's and Sons, New York, 1911.

Macdonald, Scott. Excerpt from a tenth-grade composition on Edith Wharton's *Ethan Frome,* 1975.

May, Rollo. *Love and Will.* W. W. Norton and Company, New York, 1969.

Masefield, John. "The Widow in the Bye Street." 1912.

Scott, A. C. *The Puppet Theater of Japan.* Charles E. Tuttle and Company, Rutland, Vermont and Toyko, Japan, 1963.

Schumann, R. "Widmung." 1840. Music by Schumann and poem by Friedrich Ruckert.

Sévigné, Marie de Rabutin-Chantal, Marquise de. Letter to her daughter, Mme. de Grignan, 1671.

Stein, Gertrude. *How to Write.* The Plain Edition, Paris, 1931.

Strand, Mark. "The Babies," *Reasons for Moving.* Atheneum Publishers, New York, 1968.

Tennyson, Alfred Lord. "Flower in the Crannied Wall." 1869.

Thomas, Lewis. *Lives of a Cell: Notes of a Biology Watcher.* The Viking Press, New York, 1974.

Cynthia Macdonald is the recipient of many grants and awards—among them a National Academy and Institute of Arts and Letters Award in recognition of her achievement in poetry. She was born in New York City, received her B.A. from Bennington College and her M.A. from Sarah Lawrence College. She has taught at Sarah Lawrence and Johns Hopkins University and currently directs the Creative Writing Program at the University of Houston. Cynthia Macdonald has also had a career as a singer—singing thirty-five different roles with a number of small opera companies. She has two children and lives in Houston and New York City.

A NOTE ON THE TYPE

The text of this book was set in Intertype Garamond, a modern rendering of the type first cut by Claude Garamond (1510–1561). Garamond was a pupil of Geoffroy Tory and is believed to have based his letters on the Venetian models, although he introduced a number of important differences, and it is to him we owe the letter which we know as old-style. He gave to his letters a certain elegance and a feeling of movement that won for their creator an immediate reputation and the patronage of Francis I of France.

This book was composed, printed, and bound by American Book–Stratford Press, Inc., Brattleboro, Vermont, Cornwall, New York, and Saddle Brook, New Jersey.

In her third book, in poems whose fabulous and witty surfaces astonish, Cynthia Macdonald, one of our most accomplished and elegant poets, renews her vision of the spectacle of isolation in our time. Hers is a poetry of rival circuses, of "freaks," strong-man contests, parts of the body taking precedence—then dominion, of Siamese sextuplets cut apart "to form heroic couplets," freed to "the severed bliss of being simply paired." It is a world shared by Beckett and Munch (his own paintings the moving subject of a poem: "The agonized O of the mouth / The open arms like knives, / The paint thick as spoiled cream"), a poetry of awe and riddles, a poetry sardonic and sorrowing, passionate and cool by turns.

A man loves birds, but he is afraid to go outside: "... it may rain when you are / Far away from buildings." People attend the birth of the sun:

> He was born the sun. Hair (yes, his inheritance),
> Golden corona, face, flat and luminous.
> "A clock," said the nurse

In poem after poem, as the critic Elizabeth Stone writes, "the pun is not only the poem's swivel point but the multi-chambered heart of its meaning." The grace of Cynthia Macdonald's writing, her agility, and precise visionary gifts are everywhere apparent as she illuminates the turmoils and victories of the heart in the natural struggles of life, projecting unforgettable silhouettes of defiance, longing, fortitude, simple love.